THE STORY BEHIND

MAPS

Barbara A. Somervill

Heinemann Library
Chicago, Illinois

www.heinemannraintree.com

Visit our website to find out more information about Heinemann-Raintree books.

To order:

☎ Phone 888-454-2279

🖥 Visit www.heinemannraintree.com to browse our catalog and order online.

© 2012 Heinemann Library
an imprint of Capstone Global Library, LLC
Chicago, Illinois

Visit our website at www.heinemannraintree.com

Edited by Megan Cotugno and Diyan Leake
Designed by Philippa Jenkins
Original illustrations © Capstone Global Library Ltd.
Illustrated by Oxford Designers and Illustrators
Picture research by Hannah Taylor and Mica Brancic
Production by Eirian Griffiths
Originated by Capstone Global Library
Printed in China by CTPS

15 14 13 12 11
10 9 8 7 6 5 4 3 2 1

Library of Congress Cataloging-in-Publication Data
Somervill, Barbara A.
  The story behind maps / Barbara A. Somervill.
    p. cm.—(True stories)
  Includes bibliographical references and index.
  ISBN 978-1-4329-5443-7 (hc)
  1. Maps—Juvenile literature. 2. Cartography—Juvenile literature. I. Title.
  GA105.6.S665 2012
  912—dc22   2010042106

Acknowledgments

The author and publishers are grateful to the following for permission to reproduce copyright material: © Bodleian Library p. 25; Alamy Images pp. 5 (© Illustration Works), 6, 12 (© The Art Gallery Collection), 8 (© Ivy Close Images), 9 (© Mary Evans Picture Library), 13 (© North Wind Picture Archives), 14 (© Classic Image), 22 (© Topography Resources), 24 (© Ilene MacDonald), 26 (© Michael Schmeling); Corbis pp. 11 (Steven Puetzer), 19 (Mike Agliolo); iStockphoto pp. 7 (© Steven Wynn), 23 (© Logan Dance); NASA p. 27; Shutterstock pp. 4 (© 3d brained), 10 (© Steven Wright), 18 (© Chris P), 20 (© Bubica), 21 (© Lightpoet), iii (© Sashkin); The Art Archive p. 15 (Dagli Orti).

Cover photograph of an ancient map of America reproduced with permission of Shutterstock (© Tarasenko Sergey).

We would like to thank Ann Fullick for her invaluable help in the preparation of this book.

Every effort has been made to contact copyright holders of any material reproduced in this book. Any omissions will be rectified in subsequent printings if notice is given to the publisher.

Contents

Some words are shown in bold, **like this**.
You can find out what they mean by
looking in the glossary.

Which Way Should We Go?

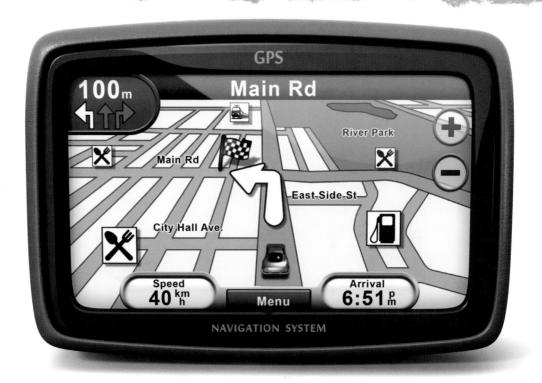

▲ GPS can tell you how to get to your destination.

Your team has a soccer game in a nearby town. You have never been to the field where you are playing before, but you can find your way. You might look up directions on the Internet or enter the address in a **Global Positioning System (GPS)** unit. Both will give you a map and easy-to-follow directions.

Maps guide you from one place to another. We use maps to find our way on roads. Trains, buses, and subways print maps of their routes. Ships follow charts, which are maps of the seas. At one time or another, we all use maps.

Today, Internet directions and GPS are high-tech maps. This technology sends signals to **satellites** high above Earth. The satellites figure out where you are and where you want to go. They plan your route and send you the directions.

Maps in the past

Getting where you want to go has not always been so easy. Fifty years ago, printed road maps were thought of as advanced technology. Mapmakers used land and road **surveys** (measurements) to produce those maps.

Just over 500 years ago, mapmakers, called **cartographers**, drew maps with much less information. They depended on information they received from travelers and sailors, but those travelers only knew what they could see. Some mapmakers looked at the **horizon**, between the sky and Earth, and believed Earth was flat. Many people—mapmakers included—thought that ships lost at sea had fallen off the edge of Earth and been swallowed by dragons!

▼ According to this map, if you fell off Earth, dragons would eat you!

The History of Mapmaking

▲ On this Babylonian world map, from about 600 BCE, the two large circles mark a great river. The rectangle is Babylon, and the circles are neighboring cultures.

two large circles

circles

rectangle

Long before people had written language, they drew pictures and maps. Over 18,000 years ago, cave dwellers in Europe drew maps on cave walls to show where they could find the animals they hunted. About 10,000 BCE, native peoples carved maps in stone in western North America.

Maps represented what people knew of the world, and so their own culture was usually at the center. Local maps showed the borders of land people owned or roads and rivers through that land.

Land maps and star charts

Greece's Anaximander (c. 610–546 BCE) was one of the first known mapmakers. He believed—as did many other Greeks—that Greece was at the center of the world, and that Earth was flat.

As Greeks advanced their understanding of mathematics, their view of the world changed. When Eratosthenes figured out Earth's **circumference**, meaning the distance around it, he proved Earth was a **sphere**, like a ball. It would take a long time for many people to believe this idea, however.

Far to the east, during the Tang dynasty (618–907 CE), Chinese **astronomers** began making detailed star charts. Star maps recorded the passage of time as the moon and stars appeared to move across the sky. The charts could be used to plan travel, particularly at sea.

Ptolemy's *Geographia*

In about 150 CE, Claudius Ptolemy (see page 12) collected many of the Greeks' ideas about **geography** in a series of eight books, called *Geographia*. Geography is the study of Earth's physical features, such as mountains, oceans, valleys, and rivers.

▶ Claudius Ptolemy (pictured left) was a skilled geographer and astronomer.

▲ Marco Polo's travels
brought Chinese
inventions, including
noodles, to Europe.

The age of exploration

In the 1200s, Italy's Marco Polo traveled to China. His journey inspired others to look to the East, a land rich with gold, silk, and, especially, spices. Pepper, cinnamon, and nutmeg spurred Europeans' desire to find a quicker route to China and the **East Indies**. To do this, explorers needed maps.

When Italian explorer Christopher Columbus set sail for the East Indies in 1492, there were already some maps that showed land on the far side of the Atlantic Ocean. After Columbus returned, other explorers, including Italian explorer Amerigo Vespucci, wanted to see the new land. Vespucci realized that Columbus's "New World" was not part of Asia, but rather a new continent.

New land meant new maps. In 1507 Dutchman Martin Waldeseemüller produced a map of South America. He used the word "America" for the first time, honoring Amerigo Vespucci.

A round planet

In 1519 Portuguese explorer Ferdinand Magellan sailed off to the Spice Islands, part of present-day Indonesia. Magellan died during the journey, but his crew returned and became the first people to travel around the world.

Europeans could no longer deny that Earth was shaped like a sphere. In 1569 cartographer Gerardus Mercator developed the Mercator **projection**, a way to draw a flat map of a round planet (see page 14).

The Vinland Map

The Vinland Map is supposed to be a map from the 1400s belonging to the Vikings, a group of Scandinavians. The map shows that Vikings set foot on North America hundreds of years before Columbus. But historians do not know if the map is real.

▼ Mercator drew this world map in 1587.

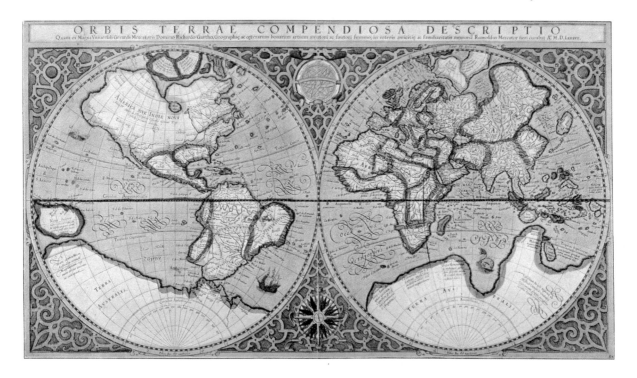

► This is an early 18th century map of North America, showing the colonies.

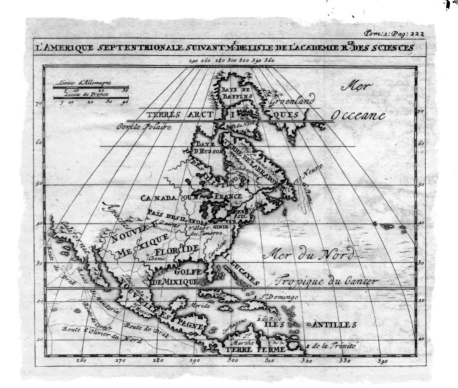

L'AMERIQUE SEPTENTRIONALE SUIVANT M. DELISLE DE L'ACADEMIE R. DES SCIENCES

Forming colonies

European nations wanted to own land in the Americas. Spain claimed most of South America, Central America, and southern North America. The French and English established large **colonies** along the east coast of North America, in the present-day United States and Canada. The Dutch held what are now New York and New Jersey. Each country mapped its newly gained land, but some borders overlapped.

Mapping colonies

Mapping continents other than Europe was a slow process. The first maps covered the coastline, drawn as explorers sailed along the coast. Rivers provided a route inland for mapping interior lands, but information was limited.

The expedition of U.S. explorers Meriwether Lewis and William Clark, from 1804 to 1806, was important in filling in the details of land west of the Mississippi River in the present-day United States.

Maps of Canada's east coast were drawn by the early 1700s, but the interior lands were not fully explored until the 1800s. The coastline around Australia was well known in the 1700s, but the interior was not accurately mapped until the late 1800s.

Technology changes mapmaking

In the early 1900s, the rising popularity of automobiles increased the need for road maps. These maps were made by traditional surveying techniques.

Mapquest, a popular online mapping service, began in 1967 as Cartographic Services—although few people had personal computers to take advantage of it. Twenty years later, GPS started to replace using surveys for mapmaking. Today, new technology allows us to get directions over cell phones and monitors in cars.

◀ Satellites send maps to us over the Internet.

Famous Mapmakers

▲ This map, drawn in 1482, was based on Ptolemy's map of the world.

Throughout history, maps have ranged from crude drawings in the dirt to works of art. There have been many great cartographers, but five of them in particular have had a major impact on mapmaking.

Claudius Ptolemy

Claudius Ptolemy (c. 85–165 CE) was a Greek mathematician, **geographer**, and astronomer who lived in Alexandria, Egypt. Ptolemy suggested that Earth was the center of the universe. He thought Earth did not move, and that the sun, moon, stars, and planets moved around Earth.

Ptolemy attempted to map the world, but his maps were not completely accurate. For instance, he drew an overly large map of Asia. Europeans believed Ptolemy's ideas about an Earth-centered universe until Copernicus, a Polish astronomer, suggested a sun-centered universe in 1543.

Muhammad ibn Muhammad al-Idrisi

Born in Morocco, in North Africa, Muhammad ibn Muhammad al-Idrisi (c. 1100–1165) studied in Spain and traveled throughout Europe. He created a 400-kilogram (880-pound) silver globe for Sicily's King Roger. Al-Idrisi's globe had seven continents, rivers, mountains, major cities, and trade routes. Al-Idrisi wrote the *Book of Roger* to explain the features on his globe. Christopher Columbus sailed across the Atlantic Ocean using a map based on one originally drawn by al-Idrisi.

Mappa Mundi

"*Mappa mundi*" means "cloth or chart of the world" and refers to world maps drawn during the Middle Ages (c. 500–1500). About 1,100 of these maps have survived from that time. The Hereford *mappa mundi* shows all rivers, towns, and features drawn within a circle.

◀ The Hereford *mappa mundi* features India as a land of 5,000 cities.

▶ Prince Henry the Navigator opened a school to teach sailors how to read maps.

Prince Henry the Navigator

Although he himself was not a mapmaker, sailing and exploring fascinated Henry, Prince of Portugal (1394–1460). Henry hoped to find sea routes to open trade with distant nations. To accomplish this, he hired explorers and mapmakers. He planned their routes, comparing new information against older maps. Henry dreamed of sailing around Africa to India. In 1498 Portuguese explorer Vasco da Gama fulfilled Henry's dream.

Gerardus Mercator

Gerardus Mercator (1512–1594) was a mathematician and geographer born in present-day Belgium. He began his mapmaking career by building a globe for Holy Roman Emperor Charles V from 1535 to 1536. (The Holy Roman Empire was a loose group of European nations ruled by Roman Catholic leaders.) A year later, Mercator published his first map, which showed Palestine and Middle Eastern cities.

14

Mercator constantly looked for new and better ways to draw maps. In 1569 he developed the Mercator Projection (see page 9), presenting the round Earth on a flat sheet of paper. We still use Mercator projection maps today.

Abraham Ortelius

Abraham Ortelius (1527–1598) was a geographer and cartographer born in Antwerp, in present-day Belgium. He published the first world **atlas**, *Theatrum Orbis Terrarum*, in 1570. Other cartographers had collections of maps, but Ortelius was the first to publish his maps in book form.

Over the past 200 years, mapmaking has undergone many advances. However, the basis of modern map work began with these five men.

▼ On Ortelius's map, Portugal and Spain are labeled as "Hispania," and France is labeled "Gallicia."

Latitude, Longitude, and Map Projections

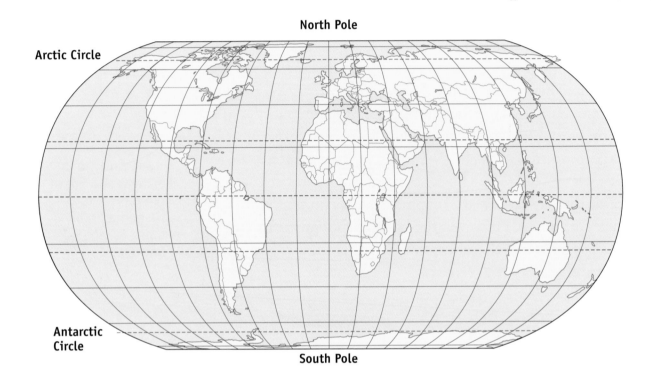

North Pole

Arctic Circle

Antarctic Circle

South Pole

▲ **Lines of latitude and longitude help people determine exact locations of places.**

Imaginary lines divide Earth into sections. Lines that run east to west are lines of **latitude**. Lines that run north to south are lines of **longitude**. Every location on Earth can be pinpointed by its latitude and longitude—the point where an east to west line meets a north to south line. Both measurements are given in degrees (°) and minutes ('), and one degree has 60 minutes.

For example, say you are looking for a point that is latitude 19° 0' north and longitude 72° 48' east. On a map or globe, begin by looking for the **equator**, an imaginary line around Earth. Find where the equator (latitude 0°) meets the **Prime Meridian** (longitude 0°).

Go north to just below latitude 20° north, then move east (to the right) along that line until you reach 72° east. Where are you? Mumbai, India!

Latitude

Degrees of latitude are measured either north or south of the equator. The number of degrees is based on an angle formed by two lines. The first runs from the equator to the center of Earth, and the second runs from the center of Earth to a point on Earth's surface.

For example, the Arctic Circle lies at latitude 66° 33' north. The angle formed from the equator to the center of Earth to the Arctic Circle is 66° 33'. All lines of latitude run parallel to the equator. The distance between two lines of latitude (1°) measures 111.4 kilometers (69.2 miles).

The equator

In 1349 Britain's Thomas Neale determined the location of the equator. The equator lies exactly halfway between the North and South **poles**. Each half of Earth is a **hemisphere**, or half a sphere. Europe, Asia, and North America lie in the northern hemisphere, while South America and Australia lie in the southern hemisphere. The equator measures 40,076 kilometers (24,902 miles).

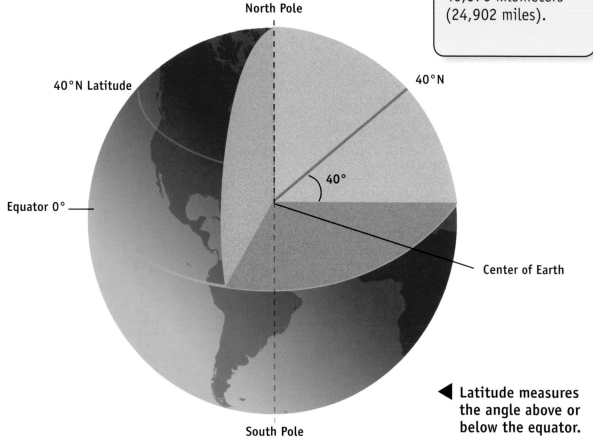

◀ Latitude measures the angle above or below the equator.

The Prime Meridian (0°) passes through Greenwich, England.

North Pole

• Greenwich

0°

Longitude

Lines of longitude run north and south on a map or globe. They are farthest apart, or widest, at the equator and meet at the North and South poles. One degree of longitude measures 111 kilometers (69 miles) at the equator and 55.5 kilometers (34.5 miles) at latitude 60°. Longitude runs 180° east and west of the line marking 0°, the Prime Meridian. All lines of longitude are called **meridians**.

Earth is also divided into 24 time zones. Time zones and lines of longitude both run north and south. However, time zones wiggle along national borders or natural boundaries, while lines of longitude are straight. The **International Date Line** lies opposite the Prime Meridian at 180°. Areas just to the left of the International Date Line are one day ahead of areas just to the right of it.

For example, say you leave California on Tuesday, heading for Tokyo, Japan. You leave at 10 a.m., and gain an hour over every time zone you pass until you reach the International Date Line. When you pass over that line, it is already Wednesday.

Map projections

A world map projection shows a round shape on a flat surface. Most map projections change the shapes of some features on the map. Some continents appear too large, while others look smaller than they are. For example, Australia is actually more than three times the size of Greenland, but it appears to be half Greenland's size on a Mercator projection. There are dozens of different map projections, but none is perfect.

▼ An "interrupted" projection looks like a globe that has been cut and laid flat.

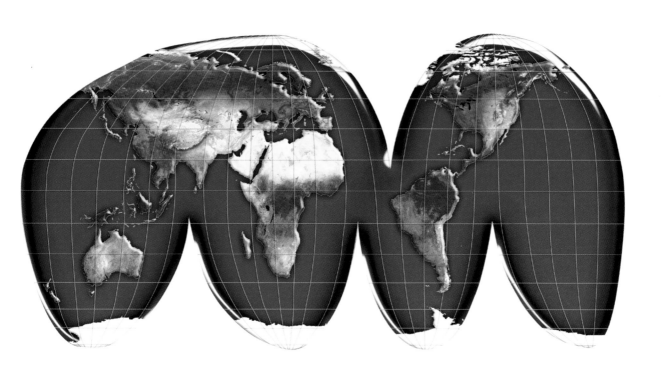

Reading a Map

▲ On a compass rose, north points toward the North Pole and, usually, the top of the map.

Reading a map is easy if you understand the various parts of a map. Typical markings on a map include **compass roses**, **scales**, and **legends** or keys.

Compass rose

Most maps have some way to tell which direction is which. Lines of latitude and longitude provide this information, as does a north-pointing arrow. A compass rose shows north, south, east, and west, as well as points in between, such as southeast or northwest. Compass roses can be fancy or simple, and the north marker points toward the geographic North Pole. Not every map has a compass rose, but all have some way to determine north.

Scales and legends

Map scales show distance. They tell you what a certain distance on the map equals on actual land. For example, on a map with a scale for which 1 inch equals 10 miles, 6.5 inches would represent 65 miles. The map of a country may have a scale of 10 centimeters to 1,000 kilometers, while the scale on a city map might be 1 centimeter to 100 meters.

A key or a legend explains the symbols on a map. Symbols could be lines, shapes, shading, colored areas, or pictures. For example, a red line on a road map might mean a single-lane road, while a double line could be a highway. Symbols on agricultural maps might show where dairy, cattle, vegetables, fruits, and grain are produced.

▼ The larger the area shown on the map, the smaller the scale of the map will be.

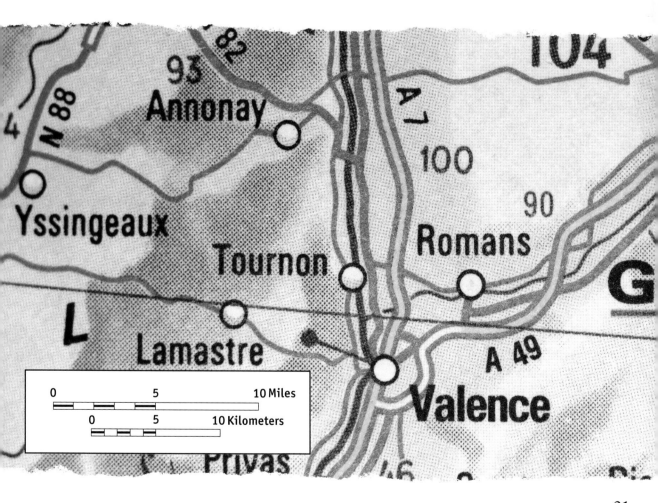

Common Types of Maps

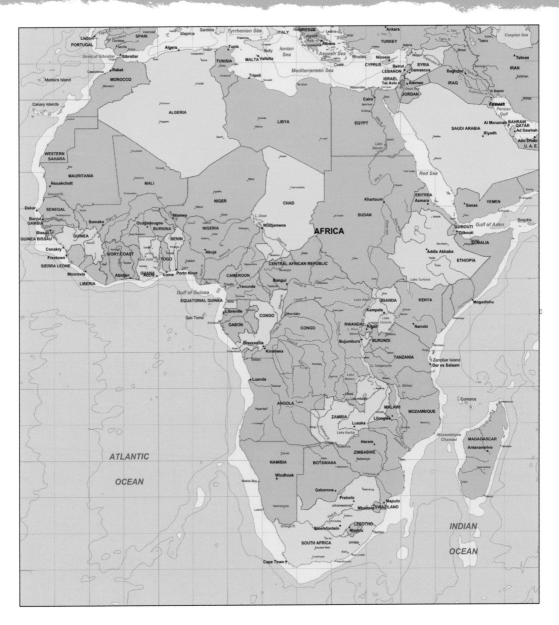

▲ As names or borders of countries change, political maps must change as well.

Different maps have different purposes. **Political** maps show the borders of countries, counties, cities, and towns. A **topographic** map shows the land features, such as mountains, lakes, or valleys. Weather maps tell us changes in weather or weather forecasts. Maps can show products or natural resources (for example, forests), roads, populations (numbers of people), and history.

Political maps

Political maps have to do with governments. They show borders and names of countries, cities, states, towns, or provinces. People rather than nature determine the features on a political map. New governments, **treaties** (agreements between nations), and wars change the national borders. For example, the continent of Africa was once divided up into European colonies. As these colonies became independent nations, many changed their names. Rhodesia, for example, became Zimbabwe.

Topographic maps

Topographic maps show land features. You can follow the paths of rivers and find lakes, seas, and oceans. These maps may show the height of a mountain and the area of a desert. Colors on topographic maps typically show land features, such as green for vegetation (plant life) and tan for deserts.

Topographic maps sometimes have legends that show what the symbols on the map mean. Others have **contour** lines, which use different lines to show places with the same height above sea level.

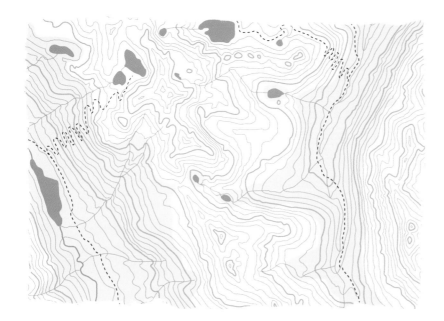

◀ This is a topographic map with blue indicating rivers and lakes.

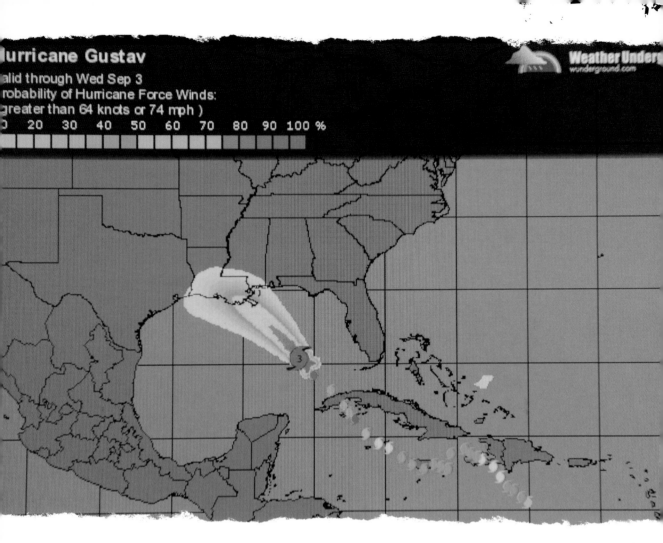

Hurricane Gustav
alid through Wed Sep 3
robability of Hurricane Force Winds:
greater than 64 knots or 74 mph)
0   20   30   40   50   60   70   80   90   100 %

Weather Under
wunderground.com

▲ This hurricane map
showed the probable
path of Hurricane
Gustav in 2008.

Weather maps

People use weather maps to learn the day's temperature,
whether it will rain or not, or if a major storm is
coming. Several different maps can be used to show
one day's weather. The first map may show high and
low temperatures, the second may show wind speeds,
while a third may show the weather you might have
tomorrow or in a few days.

An important use for weather maps is tracking
serious storms. Weather forecasters watch the paths
of tornadoes, cyclones, typhoons, and hurricanes. They
figure out how fast the storm moves, the direction it
travels, and when it may reach specific places. Weather
maps that predict the paths of storms save lives.

Road maps

Although there have been road maps since before Roman times, few individuals used to need to own maps. By the 1800s, more people traveled, roads improved, and new means of transportation were invented. By the 1900s, once many people began owning cars, they needed road maps. Road maps show major highways and the distances between locations. They also show smaller roads, roads under construction, and points of interest along the routes.

The Gough map

The Gough Map is the oldest existing road map of Great Britain. It was probably drawn in 1360. The mapmaker is unknown. Historians figured out the map's date based on changes of place names over time.

▶ No one knows who actually drew the Gough Map.

The Future of Maps

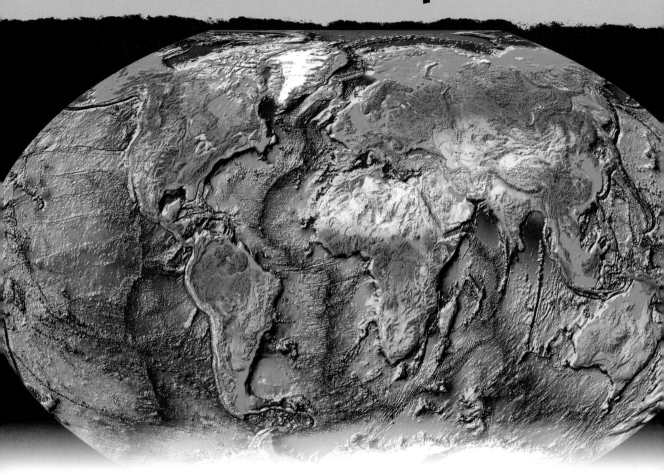

▲ This map of the ocean floor reveals that Antarctica was once surrounded by mountain ranges.

Earth changes constantly. Volcanoes erupt and build new land. Earthquakes shudder, causing land to slip into the sea. Rivers dry up or flood, and that, too, changes Earth's landscape. We build new houses, roads, and dams, and Earth is changed.

Satellites

Cartographers once relied on sailors and travelers to give them information that helped them map our world. Today, we rely on travelers of a different sort— satellites—to map Earth's landmasses. Computer-drawn maps are far more accurate and are offered over the Internet to anyone who wants one.

In the past 50 years, satellite technology has allowed us to map more than just land. For the first time, we have detailed maps of the ocean floors, with rugged mountains and plunging valleys—all underwater.

The Sloan Digital Sky Survey

Today, we map the universe on computers. The Sloan Digital Sky Survey takes pictures of millions of objects in space. Computers then measure the shape, brightness, and colors of stars and galaxies in the pictures.

This survey information produces a map that lets us figure out how big the largest formations in our universe are. It takes a long time for the light from distant stars to reach us. A star we map today may have died millions of years ago. As a result, the survey maps the past and the present of our universe at the same time.

▼ The one place left to map is space, a project being undertaken by the Sloan Digital Sky Survey.

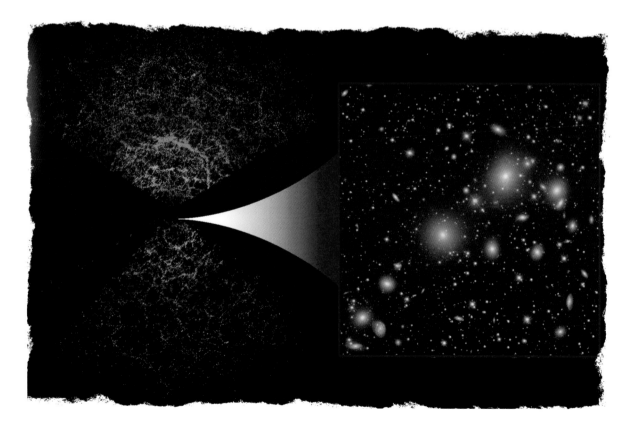

Timeline

(These dates are often approximations.)

16,000 BCE
Cave dwellers draw a map on the walls of the Lascaux caves in France.

20,000 BCE

c. 150 CE
Claudius Ptolemy writes *Geographia*, his theories of the world's geography.

200

300   400

c. 1250
The first known map of Britain is produced by Matthew Paris.

1154
Muhammad ibn Muhammad al-Idrisi draws a world map and begins writing the Book of Roger.

1200   1100

1349
Thomas Neale determines the location of the equator.

1360
The oldest existing road map of Britain is drawn.

1492
Christopher Columbus sets sail westward with a map based on the work of al-Idrisi.

1300   1400

1804-1806
William Clark makes route maps of western North America on an expedition with Meriwether Lewis.

1789
Christopher Colles produces the first road map in the United States.

1800

1867-1871
A group surveys and maps the American West.

1950s
Ivan Getting designs a basic GPS.

1900

This symbol shows where there is a change of scale in the timeline or where a long period of time with no noted events has been left out.

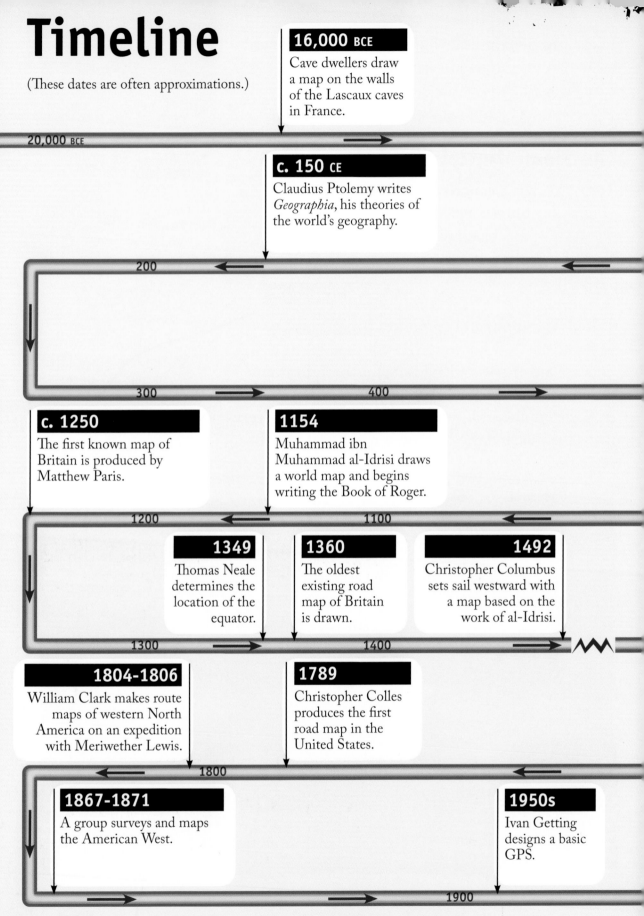

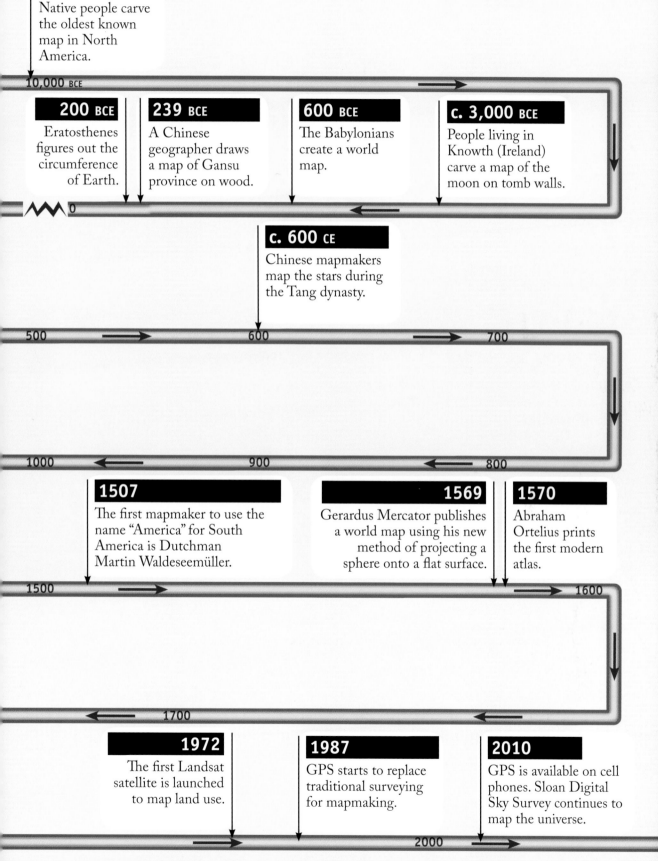

10,000 BCE
Native people carve the oldest known map in North America.

10,000 BCE

200 BCE
Eratosthenes figures out the circumference of Earth.

239 BCE
A Chinese geographer draws a map of Gansu province on wood.

600 BCE
The Babylonians create a world map.

c. 3,000 BCE
People living in Knowth (Ireland) carve a map of the moon on tomb walls.

0

c. 600 CE
Chinese mapmakers map the stars during the Tang dynasty.

500   600   700

1000   900   800

1507
The first mapmaker to use the name "America" for South America is Dutchman Martin Waldeseemüller.

1569
Gerardus Mercator publishes a world map using his new method of projecting a sphere onto a flat surface.

1570
Abraham Ortelius prints the first modern atlas.

1500   1600

1700

1972
The first Landsat satellite is launched to map land use.

1987
GPS starts to replace traditional surveying for mapmaking.

2010
GPS is available on cell phones. Sloan Digital Sky Survey continues to map the universe.

2000

Glossary

astronomer scientist who studies stars and space

atlas book of maps

cartographer mapmaker

circumference distance around the outside of a circle or sphere

colony country ruled by another, stronger country

compass rose circle divided into 8, 16, or 32 points or directions and showing which way is north

contour line joining equal points of elevation on a map

East Indies the islands in Southeast Asia

equator imaginary circle that divides Earth into northern and southern hemispheres

geographer person who studies Earth's physical features

geography study of Earth's physical features

Global Positioning System (GPS) method of determining directions to a place with the help of a satellite

hemisphere half of a sphere

horizon line appearing to be the boundary between Earth and the sky

International Date Line north-south line where the day changes, roughly 180°

latitude angular distance north or south of the equator and running parallel to it

legend table explaining symbols used on a map

longitude angular distance east or west of the Prime Meridian

meridian line on Earth's surface connecting the two poles

pole upper and lower extreme points on Earth

political of, or pertaining to, government

Prime Meridian line of longitude that is at 0°

projection method of representing Earth's features on a flat surface

satellite human-made space vehicle

scale distance on a map compared to an actual distance on Earth

sphere solid, round object

survey measure the exact boundaries, positions, and extent of land. The word is also used to describe the results of these measurements.

topographic representing land features on Earth

treaty agreement between nations

Find Out More

Books

Block, Marta Segal, and Daniel R. Block. *Mapping the World (First Guide to Maps)*. Chicago: Heinemann Library, 2008.

Dickinson, Rachel. *Tools of Navigation: A Kid's Guide to the History and Science of Finding Your Way*. White River Junction, Vt.: Nomad, 2005.

Graham, Alma. *Discovering Maps*. Springfield, N.J.: Hammond World Atlas, 2007.

Heinrichs, Ann. *Gerardus Mercator: Father of Modern Mapmaking (Signature Lives)*. Mankato, Minn.: Compass Point, 2008.

Sandvold, Rolf. *Reading Maps (All Over the Map)*. New York: Crabtree, 2009.

Websites

History of Maps and Cartography
http://academic.emporia.edu/aberjame/map/h_map/h_map.htm
Learn more about maps at this website.

U.S. National Geospatial Program: How to Make a Map
www.usgs.gov/ngpo/pdf/Maps-2s.pdf
How do you make a map? Find out at this U.S. government website.

Social Studies for Kids: The International Date Line
www.socialstudiesforkids.com/articles/geography/internationaldateline.htm
Do you want to understand more about the International Date Line? Find out more at this website.

Place to Visit

Library of Congress Map Collection
101 Independence Avenue, SE
Washington, D.C. 20540
(202) 707-8000
http://memory.loc.gov/ammem/gmdhtml/
The Geography and Map Division of the Library of Congress holds a collection of over 4.5 million items, with fascinating examples of maps from throughout history.

Index